BOOK TITLE; MARKETING LEADERSHIP-

Activate a voice & Re-activate a choice

Chapter 1; Voice discovery

Chapter 2; Voice tone

Chapter 3; Voice turning

Chapter 4; Voicing

Chapter 5; Choice discovery

Chapter 6; Investing in choice

Chapter 7; Actioning the choice

Chapter 8; Re-actioning the choice

PROVERBS 11 VERSE 26-BLESSED ARE THOSE WHO ARE WILLING TO SELL,,,,,,,

CHAPTER 1; VOICE DISCOVERY

Do you have a dream, do you have an idea. It could be a message you have for the customers. It might be a message of joy like Walt Disney-whatever. Your task is to discover it. What do you cry about, what makes you feel joy, what's the theme of your life. That will become the product you sell.

To lead in Marketing is to focus; to go within yourself first before you go without, Before you shout or say something, you have to make sure you are saying something. Let's look at the word-something. S-seek-to discover your voice in

Marketing you seek, for answers.

You do this by questioning, who do I represent, who is me, where do I come from, what am I willing to live for, and what message am I willing to do about, to share,

what's my difference, what is so rare.

O-Observe-look at your week from day one to seven-what do you talk about most, what do you do about, and you want the rest of the world to check what you do, look at your lifestyle.

M-meaning-search for meaning and draw conclusions, what does it mean, these experiences that you have encountered. To lead in Marketing is to define your own definitions, see with your own view, and you will have your own voice.

E-earnest-be earnest with yourself, be sure about yourself, and you will be sure that this is me. Be honest and you will look deep within for a voice. A product that sells is a product that rings the bells, that has something unique to say.

You must discover yours, every voice is different, but most sellers don't really discover theirs for competitive advantage. T-talk-don't keep quiet, how do you discover your ow voice in silence, share what you think you represent, and let others involved I letting you know, that oh no- this is not you.

H-for having, if you know you have a voice, you look to discover it. I-for interest, what's your excitement, it gives you a hint of your voice. N-for normal, it is seen in what you do normally with easiness. G-group-which group of people do you feel called to, which do you relate to.

CHAPTER 2; VOICE TONE

Now still on you as the product or service that is about to go out there to customers. You should know your tone of voice; that is your appeal. It is based on your personality, this is something you don't copy. You have to just know yours and use it as an asset of drawing your customers.

Are you loud and proud, are you a boaster with a thunder voice. You have a command based appeal, you take customers by surprise, by force-a forceful nature, use it, if that you.

Do you have a soft appeal, do you talk and act in a gracious way. A compassionate appeal can touch hearts of customers. To lead in Marketing, you have to discover your strength of personality and character. It was given to you, to use it in promoting your product or service.

No more trying to be what you are not, it's a waste of energy, time and resources. Are you a joker? Do you resonate well and express yourself in jokes. That will be of great impact if you use it well.

Marketing leadership is about those who are themselves, you can't really make an impact trying to be like this one or that one. That is a no, no, so you have a job of discovery again, but this time not the message, but the tone.

You don't go out there and see which tone customers love the most then you pick it.

Most product or service Marketers do that and it's a mistake. You don't pick, you discover your own personality, your own strength. Use it, everyone has it, his or her own rare and unique personhood.

If you fake it, it will be easily seen, it won't be excellent type of presentation. Those who do well are those who use their natural force of character, because they discovered it.

Originality is the thief of customers. You will steal people's hearts just by being your real self. Some tones are high-joking, boasting, and command. Some are low-emotional, compassion, gentle appeal, sympathy and empathy. WHAT'S YOURS?

CHAPTER 3; VOICE TURNING

You can't have a product or service without a target. Now we get away from you, we now focus on the customer. They say customer is King. Now you have to turn your voice according to your target.

You have to be relevant to your target. You can't be ancient and think you can sell something in this changing new-age world. What's your target market at the first place, who are you aiming your promotion to? You can't be a jack of all trades, you can't say, oh I'm aiming for everybody-that's a lame way of Marketing.

You will not win or e a leader in Marketing with that sort of view.

When you know your target, you turn your voice according to that target, its direction.

You don't choose a tone, naturally you know you are a joker, but you now have to turn those jokes to a certain direction. Make them relevant to your target.

If you are targeting Christians who range from 13-35 years old, your jokes must be not vulgar, and also must be young at heart, and this will make an impact to such type of customers. You have to achieve harmony and not be in discord.

Most people say, oh my product was born for everyone, or my service is meant for everyone-but your voice is meant for a target. People's mistake is that when they hear the word target, they think we have limited ourselves to just a few of the large market-lets hit all people.

No, there is something called focus-without focus you will be too general of a voice. This will result in lack of confidence. A general voice leads to a general choice, and then leads to a not so generous of a customer. He or she won't spend the hard earned dollars at you.

Even customers they don't just want everything, they choose. You also choose and know your target, and you turn your voice to fit and be relevant to the type that you want to impact.

CHAPTER 4; VOICING

You can't be a
Marketing leader if you

forsake planning and organizing. Now you have to speak out and practice your presentation. You now know your voice, you discovered your message, and also the personality you possess-also the target is well set.

What's next, prepare for promotion, and prepare for speech. Organize your points well. Write it down from where you are going to start and where you finish-in your promotion presentations.

You can't be haphazard, it won't come out well. Real leaders in Marketing work out their promotion strategies right behind the doors before lights, camera and action takes over the deal.

This is how you keep it real, work out your presentation, have what we call TOC-table of contents. Create the content, have your story in sequence. Title, sub –titles of presentations of your voice or your message.

Include your personality in word form, choose your words correctly based on your target. Prepare all the necessary hints, main points and best parts.

Introductions, conclusions, the punch lines, quotes and statements that will make the presentation stand out from the crowd.

Best Marketing leaders are best in planning. You must put things in order as a leader. Order makes you bolder. If things are organized, confidence is on the increase and readiness is the outcome.

Presentations that are rushed are easy to see, know that quality is also the motto in Marketing leadership. So voicing is collecting of all information, put it, group it, prepare, practice and then get ready for impact.

MARKETING

MARKETING

CHAPTER 5; CHOICE DISCOVERY

Now that your voice is ready for action, you have activated it, you now go to choice of media. You have to discover which media fits with your voice.

In discovering the media that fits, we look at all we have

discussed earlier. If your personality is that of a joker, and then the turn and target involves the young at heart, You look and see what they are using these days-YouTube, Facebook and this and that.

You then choose which one to start with first. Choose which one is going to be the main one to use in your promotions. According also to target-if it's the mature type you are targeting, they prefer also to read, so are you going to promote in a magazine or what.

It also depends on the message that you discovered. Some messages need a video presentation for them to get real meaning in customers' hearts. Also some ideas or messages can be picked well even if its audio only.

If your idea is action packed and not that analytical that involves a lot of reasoning, you cannot go with twitter or newspaper as your main media.

You have to choose a media that gives you a platform to perform in action so that the customers will see what you are saying visibly.

MARKETING

MARKETING

MARKETING

CHAPTER 6;
INVESTING IN CHOICE

Now as a Marketer, you have to know your

budgeting, cost of promotion and cost of the media choice. See if you are prepared beforehand to invest in what's needed.

These days, there is social media, which is a cheap and impactful way of Marketing your products and services. Consider and use these.

Yes it might be cheap but make sure you don't compromise on the quality. It is going to cost you something, check the equipment you are to use to post videos for promotion. You must look at the image that you want to set. Marketing leaders must set a high standard, and be an example of a quality image.

Most Marketers think it's just simple and

straight forward, you just post anything as long as your message and appeal resonates with customers, but, no, you have to be creative, and there is going to be an expense you have to cover to come up with something real.

Quality always will cost you something, be prepared, and have a budget you are working with. That's why some Marketers pay a huge amount of money to involve celebrities, because they enhance the quality of their

appeal. This makes their voice to be heard differently than usual.

MARKETING

MARKETING

MARKETING

MARKETING

CHAPTER 7; ACTIONING THE CHOICE

Now just do it, put action and promote your idea, your product, and your service. Do it, don't hesitate, you have prepared, you have planned and you have gone through the process.

Do it now, don't postpone to when, you will not do it then. Now is the time to lead in Marketing, to reach your target market, to shock them, surprise them and touch them in unique ways.

It takes energy to action the promotion. Appearance is where you appear, its energy used- the force of nature. Be somewhere and change your place.

Be there and be found, customers are searching, let them meet you in their search. Let them proclaim and declare that, Yes, this is me, when you have shared your story in the content of your presentation.

Let them identify with your product or service, so you have to make a shift. A change of energy is a change of reality. Why are you sleeping with your idea, your voice, make it be heard.

What's inside must now come out, do it now and think later. What you feel that you are, what you think that you are, and what you have discovered that you are must match with what people see now on the outside.

There must be no conflict, don't just know it and not show it. Those who do it are the better, they learn as they do, they adjust their strategy and do it again.

MARKETING

MARKETING

MARKETING

CHAPTER 8; RE-ACTIONING THE CHOICE

If video media was your choice, why is it only one video in your name? Look at others, they have more, they reach to 100 plus videos. What are they doing- they are re-actioning their choice of media.

They are being consistent in their quest for customers. They are building a following through their many presentations. We call it faithfulness.

Customers have a habit of wanting more and more-an abundance habit. You have a voice but you speak less, no, that's a lame leadership strategy.

Re-action your choice to be a Marketing leader. Quantify your content. A healthy child you can see his development by the amount of words. First he speaks only one, in time a sentence comes out of his mouth.

The parents expects that from a child. Let me tell you that the customers also expect that from you. They want to know what's happening, what's next, what's for today and what's for the future. Let them know, continue and be loyal to your choice of media. Be in the increase, you will perfect as you grow. Grow in your choice by re-actioning that choice-YOU ARE A MARKETING LEADER ,,,The Kingdom of God like a seed and growth to a big tree.

MARKETING

MARKETING

www.ingramcontent.com/pod-product-compliance
Lightning Source LLC
Chambersburg PA
CBHW031113180526
45163CB00011B/2040